This
BOOK
belongs to:

_____

To read with:

_____

For Emma, Elsie and Emile – M.R.

For my parents, and all the times my brother and I went mad in the back! – R.W.

PICTURE SQUIRRELS

Published in 2015 in Great Britain by Barrington Stoke Ltd
18 Walker Street, Edinburgh, EH3 7LP

www.picturesquirrels.co.uk

This story was first published in a different form in *The Hypnotiser* (André Deutsch, 1988)

Text © 1988 Michael Rosen
Illustrations © 2015 Richard Watson

A CIP catalogue record for this book is available from the British Library upon request

ISBN 978-1-78112-509-0

Printed in China

Michael ROSEN & Richard WATSON

Mad IN THE Back

PICTURE SQUIRRELS

Mum says, "Right, you two, this is a very long car journey. I want you two to be good. I'm driving and I can't drive properly if you two are going mad in the back. Do you understand?"

So we say, "OK, Mum, OK. Don't worry."

And off we go.

And we start The Moaning.

"Can I have a drink?" "I want some crisps." "Can I open my window?"

"He's got my book."

"Get off me." "Ow, that's my ear!"

And Mum tries to be exciting. "Look out the window – there's a lamp-post."

And we go on with The Moaning.

"Can I have a sweet?" "He's sitting on me." "Are we nearly there?"

"Don't scratch." "You never tell him off." "Now he's biting his nails."

"I want a drink."

"I want a drink."

And Mum tries to be exciting again. "Look out the window – there's a tree."

And we go on. "My hands are sticky."

"He's playing with the door handle now."

"I feel sick."

"Your nose is all runny."

"Don't pull my hair."

"He's punching me, Mum. That's really dangerous, you know. Mum, he's spitting."

And Mum says, "Right, I'm stopping the car. I AM STOPPING THE CAR."

She stops the car.

"Now, if you two don't stop it I'm going to put you out of the car and leave you by the side of the road."

"She started it."

"I didn't. He started it."

"I don't care who started it. I can't drive properly if you two go mad in the back. Do you understand?"

And we say, "OK, Mum, OK, don't worry."

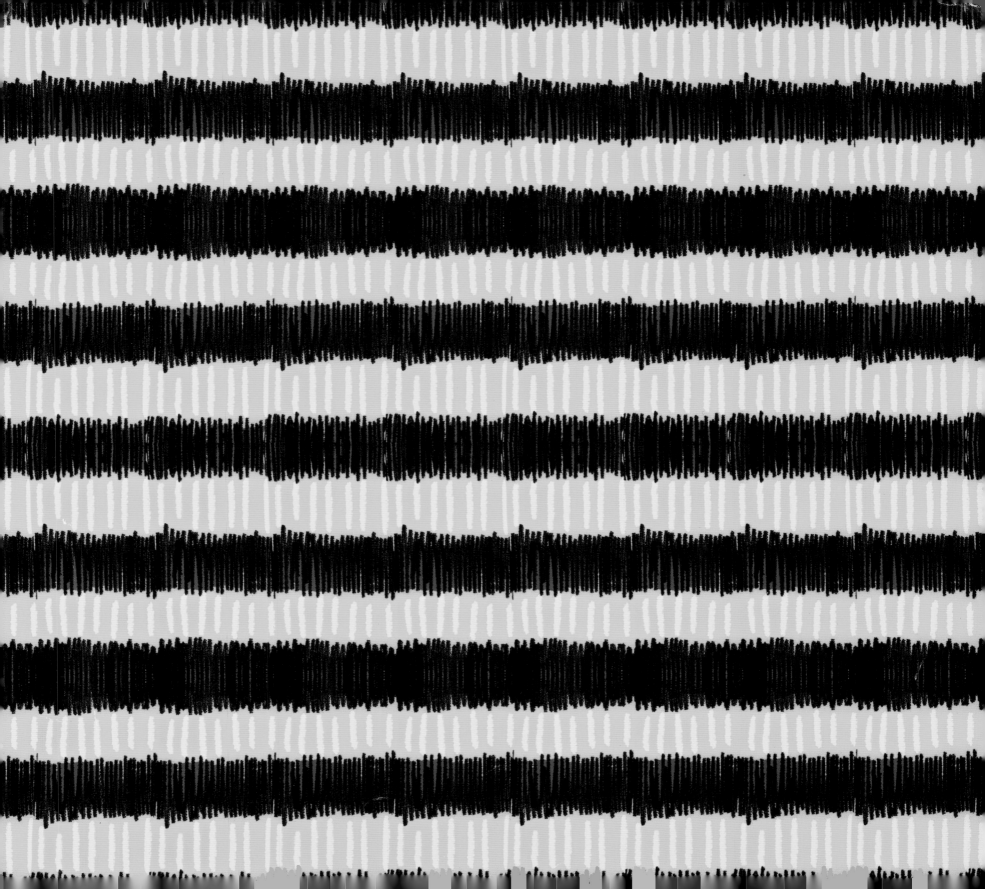

Vroom! Vroom!

Help Mum find her way home.

Trace the road with your finger to find the way!

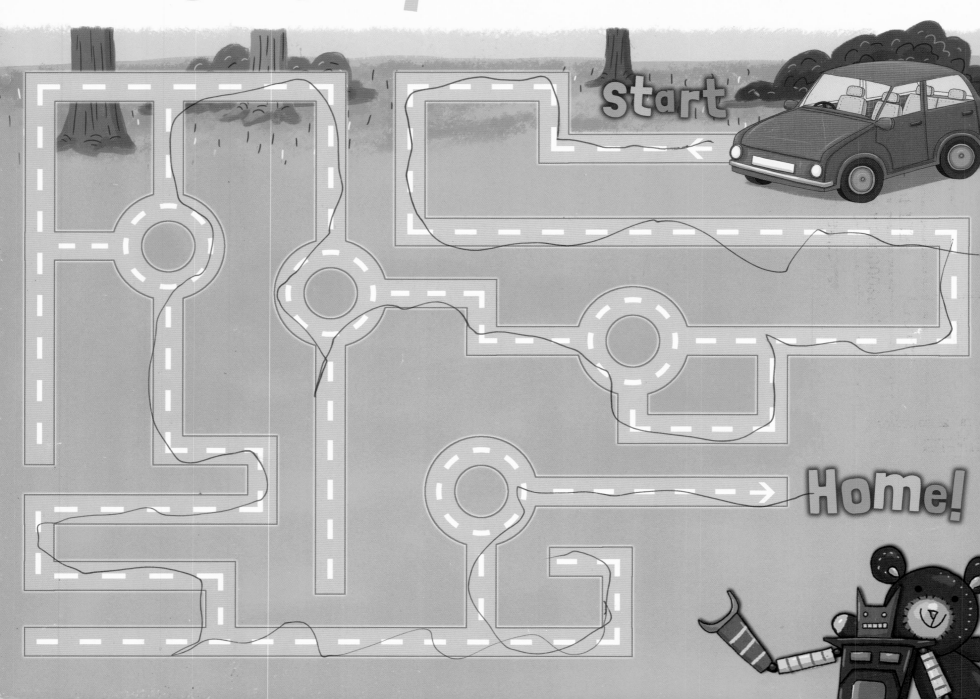

Start

Home!